NBA CHAMPIONSHIPS:

↓

1994, 1995

↓

ALL-TIME LEADING SCORER:

↓

HAKEEM OLAJUWON (1984–2001):

↓

26,511 POINTS

THE NBA:
A HISTORY OF HOOPS

HOUSTON ROCKETS

BY JIM WHITING

CREATIVE EDUCATION CREATIVE PAPERBACKS

Published by Creative Education
and Creative Paperbacks

P.O. Box 227, Mankato, Minnesota 56002

Creative Education and Creative Paperbacks
are imprints of The Creative Company

www.thecreativecompany.us

Design and production by Blue Design
Printed in the United States of America

Photographs by Corbis (Bettmann, Song Qiong/
Xinhua Press), Getty Images (Bill Baptist/NBAE,
Andrew D. Bernstein/NBAE, Nathaniel S. Butler/
NBAE, Ronald Cortes/Getty Images Sport, Jim
Cummins/NBAE, James Drake/Sports Illustrated,
Stephen Dunn/Getty Images Sport, Noah Graham/
NBAE, Mark Green, Thearon W. Henderson/Getty
Images Sport, George Long/Sports Illustrated,
John W. McDonough/Sports Illustrated, Fernando
Medina/NBAE, Dick Raphael/NBAE, Kyle Terada/
Pool), Newscom (imago sportfotodienst)

Library of Congress Cataloging-in-Publication Data

Names: Whiting, Jim, 1943- author.

Title: Houston Rockets / Jim Whiting.

Series: The NBA: A History of Hoops.

Includes bibliographical references and index.

Summary: This high-interest title summarizes
the history of the Houston Rockets professional
basketball team, highlighting memorable events
and noteworthy players such as Hakeem Olajuwon.

Identifiers: LCCN 2016054010 / ISBN 978-1-60818-
845-1 (hardcover) / ISBN 978-1-62832-448-8
(pbk) / ISBN 978-1-56660-893-0 (eBook)

Subjects: LCSH: 1. Houston Rockets
(Basketball team)—History—Juvenile
literature. 2. Houston Rockets (Basketball
team)—Biography—Juvenile literature.

Classification: LCC GV885.52.H68 W45 2017 /
DDC 796.323/64097641411—dc23

CCSS: RI.4.1, 2, 3, 4; RI.5.1, 2, 4; RI.6.1, 2,
3; RF.4.3, 4; RF.5.3, 4; RH. 6-8. 4, 5, 7

First Edition HC 9 8 7 6 5 4 3 2 1

First Edition PBK 9 8 7 6 5 4 3 2 1

CONTENTS

LEGENDS OF THE HARDWOOD

The largest city in Texas, **HOUSTON** is home to pro teams in four major sports.

FROM SHADOW TO SPOTLIGHT

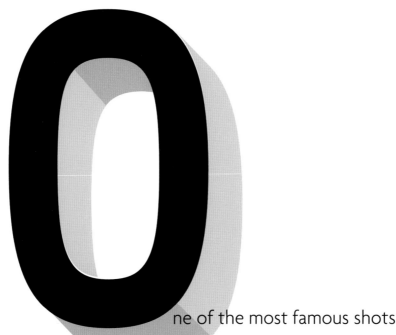

One of the most famous shots in Houston Rockets history came from a little-known player. The Rockets faced the Phoenix Suns in the second round of the 1995 National Basketball

MARIO ELIE'S famous
3-pointer emphasized Houston's
nickname as "Clutch City."

Association (NBA) playoffs. The deciding Game 7 was tied at 110 in the final moments. Houston guard Mario Elie had the ball far from the basket. He was hardly a star. The Rockets were the fourth team in his six-year career. Everyone thought he would pass the ball to Houston's best player, center Hakeem "The Dream" Olajuwon. Elie had other ideas. "Dream was wide open, but I had my feet set," Elie said. "I let it go, and it felt good." The three-pointer dropped through the net with seven seconds remaining. "Super Mario" blew a goodbye kiss to the Suns' bench. The Rockets won, 115–114. They went on to capture the NBA title.

The Rockets' story began in 1967. The NBA expanded to Seattle and San Diego. Many people regarded San Diego as the "poor relative" of the more famous California cities of San Francisco and Los Angeles. San Diego officials wanted to increase awareness of their city. They had just adopted the motto "A city in motion." Nothing screamed "motion" more than the powerful Atlas rockets. They carried the country's first astronauts into space. The Atlas was manufactured in San Diego. Many aerospace companies dotted the region. "Rockets" was an appropriate nickname for the new franchise. But the team struggled to lift off in its first season. The roster was a mix of untested rookies and veterans other teams didn't want. The Rockets finished 15–67. It was an NBA record for most losses in a season.

12

MY TWO LEFT SHOES

ELVIN HAYES, POWER FORWARD, 6-FOOT-9, 1968–72

Elvin Hayes grew up in rural Mississippi. In eighth grade, he was wrongly blamed for a classroom prank. A teacher thought playing basketball would help his development. "I didn't own shoes from first grade to ninth grade," he said. "Whenever I had to go someplace, I would borrow shoes from a cousin." Hayes found two left tennis shoes in the trash. He taped them to his feet. He was clumsy. His teammates laughed at him. Hayes was determined to get better. As a high school senior, Hayes averaged 35 points a game. His team won the state championship. No one laughed at him anymore.

T here was one consolation. The Rockets "earned" the first pick in the 1968 NBA Draft. They chose powerful forward Elvin Hayes. The "Big E" lived up to expectations. He averaged more than 28 points and 17 rebounds a game. "Rebounding is a rough proposition," he said. "But it's one of the ways I make my living, so it's something I force myself to tolerate, no matter how many bruises I wind up with." Incredibly, Wes Unseld of the Baltimore Bullets beat Hayes for Rookie of the Year honors. The Rockets went 37–45. They qualified for the playoffs. They lost in the first round to the Atlanta Hawks, four games to two. San Diego fell to a 27–55 record the following year. The Rockets struck gold twice in the 1970 NBA Draft. They chose burly forward Rudy Tomjanovich in the first round. They selected guard Calvin Murphy in the second round. Along with Hayes, the newcomers boosted the Rockets to 40–42 in the 1970–71 season. They fell just short of the playoffs.

FOLLOWING MOSES

San Diego may have been a "city in motion." But few people moved toward Rockets games. The owners were discouraged by poor attendance and losing records. They sold the team.

The smallest player in the league, **CALVIN MURPHY** relied on speed and sharp shooting.

Forward **ELVIN HAYES** developed a turnaround jump shot to score over opponents.

Houston businessman Wayne Duddlesten led the new ownership group. When the team moved to Houston, there was no question about keeping the name. NASA's Manned Spacecraft Center had been headquartered in Houston since 1961. The city was known for the enormous rockets that carried astronauts into space. The sale became final just a few weeks before the opening of the 1971–72 season. There was no time to find a permanent home. The Rockets had to split their games among

LEGENDS OF THE HARDWOOD

TOO SMALL? NOT!

CALVIN MURPHY, GUARD, 5-FOOT-9, 1970—83

Calvin Murphy's first love was basketball. He used to watch professional games. He imagined himself on the court. There was one problem. He was "too short." At least that was what people told him. He didn't believe them. "He was like a bantamweight who dared to make his living in the heavyweight division," said teammate Major Jones. Murphy was named to the All-Rookie Team when he joined the Rockets. He averaged nearly 18 points a game in his career. He still holds the Houston record for assists with 4,402. As of 2017, Murphy is one of just six Rockets to have his number retired.

Guard **MIKE NEWLIN** was a reliable force for eight seasons in Houston.

several arenas in Houston. They also played some "home games" out of town. The Rockets traveled to Waco and San Antonio, Texas, for games. Albuquerque, New Mexico, became another "home." They even played twice back in San Diego. The team was hardly an instant hit in its new city. Average attendance was just 4,966. A game in Waco attracted only 759 spectators. The radio broadcasters of that game added pre-recorded crowd noise to make it sound more exciting.

There was another problem. New coach Tex Winter said, "Even though Elvin [Hayes] was an All-Star, the truth was that he had the worst fundamentals of any player I've ever coached." Winter traded Hayes to Baltimore. Houston struggled. Led by Tomjanovich and Murphy, Houston improved to 41–41 in 1974–75. The Rockets shocked the favored New York Knicks in the first round of the playoffs. But the Boston Celtics defeated Houston in the next round.

Powerhouse **MOSES MALONE** led the league in rebounding three times with Houston.

The team's improved play attracted more fans. So did massive center Moses Malone. He went directly from high school to the rival American Basketball Association (ABA) in 1974. He joined the Rockets two years later when the ABA folded. Malone gave Houston a strong inside presence. He displayed powerful rebounding and shot-blocking. Also new that season was point guard John Lucas. He was the top overall selection of the 1976 NBA Draft. "John doesn't overwhelm you with talent," said teammate Mike Newlin. "He's just smooth. He asserts himself without infringing on anyone else's space, which is really an art."

Houston surged to 49–33 in 1976–77. It was the first winning record in franchise history. The Rockets faced the Bullets and Hayes in the first round of the playoffs. Houston won in six games. But it couldn't get past the Philadelphia 76ers in the next round. Fans had

RUDY TOMJANOVICH (45) and MALONE (24) launched the Rockets to the 1981 Finals.

22

high hopes for the following season. The Rockets played the Los Angeles Lakers in early December. A fight broke out during the game. The Lakers' Kermit Washington punched Tomjanovich so hard that he missed the rest of the season. Without his scoring and leadership, Houston went into a tailspin. The Rockets finished just 28–54. They rebounded to 47–35 the following season. Malone averaged nearly 25 points and 18 rebounds a game. He was named Most Valuable Player (MVP). But the Atlanta Hawks eliminated the Rockets in the first round of the playoffs. Houston dropped to 41–41 the next season. It beat the San Antonio Spurs in the first round of the playoffs. But Boston shot down the Rockets in the second round.

23

LEGENDS OF THE HARDWOOD

THE PUNCH

HOUSTON ROCKETS VS. LOS ANGELES LAKERS, DECEMBER 9, 1977

During the game, the Rockets' Kevin Kunnert got into a fight with Lakers forward Kermit Washington. Rockets forward Rudy Tomjanovich tried to break it up. Washington smashed him in the face. Tomjanovich nearly died. He needed extensive surgery. He made a remarkable return to the court in the 1978–79 season. He averaged 19 points and 7.7 rebounds per game. He retired two years later. The NBA suspended Washington for two months. He went on to have a 10-year career. He played in the 1979–80 All-Star Game. But most fans remember him only for "The Punch."

ERECTING THE TWIN TOWERS

No one expected anything from the Rockets when the 1980–81 regular season ended. They squeezed into the playoffs with a 40–42 record. Then they caught fire. They beat Los Angeles

25

Towering big men **RALPH SAMPSON** and **HAKEEM OLAJUWON** made a wall at the basket.

A dependable scorer, **ROBERT REID** also defended against top-scoring opponents.

"I REALLY BELIEVED THAT HOUSTON WAS GOING TO WIN THE COIN FLIP, AND I REALLY WANTED TO PLAY IN HOUSTON, SO I HAD TO MAKE THAT DECISION."

2–1 in the first round. They knocked off the Spurs 4–3 in the second round. They blasted the Kansas City Kings 4–1 in the Western Conference finals. Houston became just the second team with a losing record to compete for the NBA championship. Then the magic ran out. Boston defeated the Rockets four games to two. Houston won 46 games next season. However, it didn't make it past the first playoffs round. Malone was the league's MVP again. But Houston traded him before the 1982–83 season. The Rockets ran out of fuel. They plunged to 14–68. It was their worst-ever record.

Houston had the top pick in the 1983 NBA Draft. Team officials chose 7-foot-4 center Ralph Sampson. He averaged 21 points, 11.1 rebounds, and 2.4 blocks per game. He also earned Rookie of the Year honors. The Rockets drafted small forward Rodney McCray, too. Both players helped Houston improve to 29–53 their first season. Yet the team still finished last in the Western Conference. The Rockets struck it rich in the 1984 NBA Draft. University of Houston superstar center Hakeem Olajuwon was a junior in college. He had to decide whether to return for his senior year or enter the draft. The worst teams in the two NBA conferences flipped a coin to decide which one would have the top choice. Olajuwon said, "I really believed that Houston was going to win the coin flip, and I really wanted to play in Houston, so I had to make that decision" [to leave early]. He guessed right. Houston won the toss.

Some wondered if Houston needed two 7-footers. Not coach Bill Fitch. "I don't know a coach who would tell you that Olajuwon and Sampson can't play together in the same lineup," Fitch said. "Then again, we could cut them in half and make four guards." The "Twin Towers" helped the Rockets soar to 48–34. They lost to the Utah Jazz in the first round of the playoffs.

Houston notched a franchise-best 51 wins in 1985–86. The Rockets roared through the first three rounds of the playoffs. They lost to Boston in the NBA Finals, four games to two. Fans looked forward to repeating that success. They were disappointed. Trades, injuries, and off-court problems hampered the Rockets. "We didn't know it, but our window was right there, and then it slammed shut," Lucas said years later. The Rockets enjoyed winning records in five of the next six seasons. They always sputtered in the playoffs. Rudy Tomjanovich took over as coach during the 1991–92 season. Rookie small forward Robert Horry became an immediate starter in 1992. Houston shot to its best-ever season, winning 55 games. The team suffered a heartbreaking defeat in Game 7 of the Western Conference semifinals, losing to Seattle 103–100. "It's tough losing close ones," said Horry, "but it shows how close we are."

29

DAWN OF THE DREAM

HAKEEM "THE DREAM" OLAJUWON, CENTER, 7 FEET, 1984–2001

Oliver B. Johnson wanted to introduce basketball in the African country of Nigeria. While he was there, he met Hakeem Olajuwon. "Want to shoot some hoops?" Johnson asked. "No. I play soccer and team handball," Olajuwon replied. Soon, he turned up at the gym where Johnson was coaching the Nigerian national team. Johnson put him on the team. Later, the University of Houston recruited Olajuwon to play for them. The coaches had him work out with Moses Malone, the imposing Rockets' center. "The way Moses helped me is by being out there playing and allowing me to go against that level of competition," he said.

OLAJUWON racked up 35 points per game against the Spurs in the 1995 playoffs.

31

BLASTING OFF TO THE TITLE

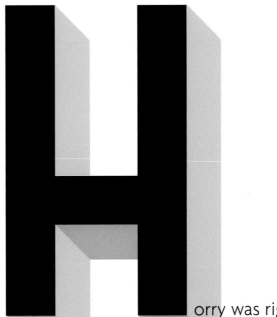

orry was right. Houston
won 58 games in 1993–94. Olajuwon averaged 27 points
and 12 rebounds. He blocked nearly four shots a game.
He was named MVP and Defensive Player of the Year.

Guard **CLYDE DREXLER** was called "The Glide" for the way he soared to the hoop.

Houston faced the New York Knicks for the NBA championship. In a closely played series, New York took a 3–2 edge. The Rockets escaped with an 86–84 win in Game 6. Olajuwon blocked a last-second three-pointer. He scored 25 points in Game 7. This launched the Rockets to a 90–84 win. It was their first NBA title! Olajuwon was named series MVP. "This was a tough battle," he said. "It was truly a championship game. If you write a book, you can't write it any better."

32

Though the Rockets dropped to 47 wins the following year, their playoff performance continued at the highest level. A midseason trade for shooting guard Clyde Drexler added scoring power. Drexler had been Olajuwon's college teammate. Elie's last-second shot helped defeat Phoenix in the second round. The Rockets beat San Antonio in the conference finals. They faced the Orlando

34

LEARNING FROM THE BEST

YAO MING, CENTER, 7-FOOT-6, 2002–11

Starting when he was 17, Yao Ming played professionally in China. But that didn't really prepare him for the NBA. After Ming's rookie season, the Rockets hired Hall-of-Fame center Patrick Ewing to work with him. A year later, defensive specialist Dikembe Mutombo joined the team. He contributed to Ming's development. So did Hakeem Olajuwon. He taught Ming how to be more effective under the basket. All those lessons paid off. Ming completed his Rockets' career with averages of 19 points, 9 rebounds, and 2 blocked shots per game. He was an eight-time All-Star.

Forward **ROBERT HORRY** was one of the best performers when the game was on the line.

Magic in the NBA Finals. Houston swept the series, 4–0. The Rockets repeated as champs! Olajuwon repeated as series MVP. "We had nonbelievers all along the way, and I have one thing to say to those nonbelievers: Don't ever underestimate the heart of a champion," said Tomjanovich. The Rockets hoped to become only the fourth team to win three titles in a row. Seattle had other plans. The SuperSonics swept Houston in the second round of the 1995–96 playoffs. Houston came close to another title the following season. It won 57 games and advanced to the Western Conference finals. But the Rockets lost to the Jazz 4–2. They made the playoffs again the next two seasons. Both times they fizzled in the first round.

At 7-foot-6, center **YAO MING** hauled in plenty of rebounds, but he could also shoot.

YAO MING HAD NEVER PLAYED
IN THE UNITED STATES. "IT WILL
TAKE TIME TO ADAPT," HE SAID,
"BUT I THINK I CAN HANDLE IT."

The next three seasons, Houston missed the playoffs. One bright spot was speedy guard Steve Francis. He was named co-Rookie of the Year in 2000. Then, Olajuwon left the team before the 2001–02 season. The Rockets won just 28 games. That poor record gave them the first overall choice in the 2002 NBA Draft. They took 7-foot-6 Chinese center Yao Ming. He had never played in the United States. "It will take time to adapt," he said, "but I think I can handle it." Ming helped the Rockets improve to 43–39. They missed the playoffs by just one game. He became the first rookie in eight years to start in the All-Star Game. He finished second in Rookie of the Year voting.

38

m&m ... AND MORE

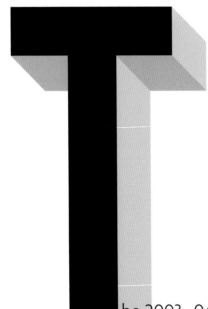

The 2003–04 season began on a sad note. Tomjanovich was diagnosed with cancer. He resigned. That ended his 33-year association with the team. The Rockets returned to the playoffs with a 45–37

Forward **TRACY "T-MAC" McGRADY** possessed a rare combination of size and skills.

AN EPIC COMEBACK

HOUSTON ROCKETS VS. SAN DIEGO CLIPPERS, GAME 6, WESTERN CONFERENCE SEMIFINALS, SAN DIEGO, CALIFORNIA, MAY 14, 2015

San Diego had taken a 3–1 series lead. Houston won at home in Game 5. The series returned to San Diego for Game 6. The Clippers led by 19 late in the third quarter. "It's easy to give in and just say, 'Maybe next year,'" said James Harden. "But I think the injuries throughout the entire year kind of made us fight through adversity no matter what." The Rockets outscored San Diego 40–15 in the fourth quarter. They won 119–107. They also won Game 7. Houston became only the ninth team in NBA history to overcome a 3–1 series deficit.

Known for his bushy beard, **JAMES HARDEN** was an explosive scorer and four-time All-Star.

record. They lost to the Lakers in the first round. A trade brought small forward/shooting guard Tracy McGrady to Houston. He became an All-Star several times during his Houston career. Ming and McGrady helped Houston win more than 50 games in four of the next five seasons. Each time, they left the playoffs early. The Rockets made the Western Conference semifinals in 2008–09. They fell to the Lakers in seven games. The next three seasons were difficult for Houston. McGrady and Ming suffered major injuries. The Rockets barely posted winning marks.

42

The Rockets worked together to reach 43 wins in 2010–11 but fell short of the playoffs.

Before the 2012–13 season, Houston added shooting guard James Harden through a trade with the Oklahoma City Thunder. He scored 37 points in his first Rockets game. Harden became noted for the number of free throws he was awarded. "I'm not necessarily going in there and trying to draw a foul," he said. "But if a person can't guard you, he has to foul you. Every. Single. Time." Houston improved to 45–37. They returned to the playoffs for the first time in four years. They lost to the Thunder in the first round. The following season, superstar center Dwight Howard

HARDEN poured in 26.6 points per game against the Warriors in the 2016 playoffs.

chose Houston over four other teams. The Rockets soared to 54–28 but couldn't get past the first round of the playoffs. Houston wouldn't be denied the following year. After winning 56 games, it blasted through the first two rounds of the playoffs. But it lost to Golden State 4–1 in the conference finals. The Warriors had completed one of the greatest seasons in NBA history, winning 67 games. The Rockets returned to the playoffs with just 41 wins in 2015–16. But the Warriors were back, too. They bounced Houston out in the first round.

Combining Harden's MVP-worthy play with new coach Mike D'Antoni's skillful orchestration, the Rockets blasted to a 55–27 mark in 2016–17. They defeated the Thunder in the first round of the playoffs. But with a chance to tie the conference semifinal series against San Antonio, the Rockets instead tumbled to an embarrassing 114–75 loss to end their season.

The Rockets have lived up to their name during their years in the NBA. They combined some of the tallest players in league history with explosive scoring. Houston fans fully expect their team to remain in the championship hunt for years to come.

SELECTED BIBLIOGRAPHY

Ballard, Chris. *The Art of a Beautiful Game: The Thinking Fan's Tour of the NBA*. New York: Simon & Schuster, 2010.

Hareas, John. *Ultimate Basketball: More Than 100 Years of the Sport's Evolution*. New York: DK, 2004.

Hubbard, Jan, ed. *The Official NBA Basketball Encyclopedia*. 3rd edition. New York: Doubleday, 2000.

NBA.com. "Houston Rockets." http://www.nba.com/rockets/.

Simmons, Bill. *The Book of Basketball: The NBA According to the Sports Guy*. New York: Ballantine, 2009.

Sports Illustrated. *Sports Illustrated Basketball's Greatest*. New York: Sports Illustrated, 2014.

WEBSITES

CLUTCH'S CORNER
http://www.nba.com/rockets/clutch/clutch_corner.html

Visit this Houston Rockets kids site centered on the team mascot, Clutch.

JR. NBA
http://jr.nba.com/

This kids site has games, videos, game results, team and player information, statistics, and more.

Note: Every effort has been made to ensure that any websites listed above were active at the time of publication. However, because of the nature of the Internet, it is impossible to guarantee that these sites will remain active indefinitely or that their contents will not be altered.

INDEX